TRANSLATIONS FROM THE FLESH

PITT POETRY SERIES
Ed Ochester, Editor

Translations from the Flesh

◉ ◉ ◉

ELTON GLASER

University of Pittsburgh Press

Published by the University of Pittsburgh Press, Pittsburgh, Pa., 15260
Copyright © 2013, Elton Glaser
Manufactured in the United States of America
Printed on acid-free paper
10 9 8 7 6 5 4 3 2 1
ISBN 13: 978-0-8229-6234-2
ISBN 10: 0-8229-6234-9

for Charles Wright and the late Donald Justice
from whom I am still learning

the heart breaks and breaks
and lives by breaking.

—Stanley Kunitz

CONTENTS

One

Two

Three

⊙ ONE

Love is not mocked whatever use you put it to.
—JACK SPICER

Eastern Winter Time

I was entirely asleep, moon at my window
Like a burglar come to steal the darkness inside.

Letting go of everything—that was Buddha's dream, not mine.
Mine was to hang on by the slippery tip of each finger,

Even if the rain blew sideways in a bloat of wind
Like the swarmy voices of the Mormon Tabernacle Choir.

Mine was to scratch a living from the empty page,
Not to proofread suicide notes before the blood dried.

Did it matter when I woke? For my alarm,
I should buy an hourglass cramped with snow.

Out in the hunter's dark, the stars glared down at me.
But the heart is a moving target.

Evenings Homesick for the Absolute

The day turns in its half circle, east to west,
Wheel that grinds the hours
Down to shadow and after, spindly twins of the dead.

From noon on, I could hear the wind thinking out loud,
Panic of vernacular
Through the long wires and hard sky.

I could lip-read the leaves, in their curl and twist:
Wait. It's not over. A last inch of revelation
Will still unroll.

Orphan of the lost beliefs, I want to
Feel those words warm me, the way the sun
Mothers up the new blooms.

I want a second chance at the absolute,
Wherever it is, whatever it is,
The late years creaking through me like a pack mule.

Inside, candles sniff the air for a dark scent;
Amber of brandy holds its own glow. All over town, the lamps
Go on, go out, like random firings in the brain,

And stars set off their neons of permission,
Hot blink at the end of the odd:
Vacancy. Room to let.

And room enough for me, too, if sleep,
Like St. Christopher, would
Carry me on its back to the other shore.

But who lives on moon soup or bread
Handed down from thin women? Refugees from the real;
Pilgrims paring themselves to pure bone.

I mop my plate with coarse crusts
And lick the spoon. I know too much of exile
To disappear into myself—

Even in this raw dark, slow and cold,
I leave my windows open for
The vast eccentric innocence of light.

Regression Analysis

Back to the sleepy years, rise
Of the rear fin and the crenelated pompadour,

Moon like a hubcap rolling loose
In a night sky, more sex than science,

Beyond the evils of geometry at three in the afternoon,
Back to the long muscles born out of sweat and throb,

Soft hair cradling a face at the sock hop,
The nudge of new breasts under blouse and arousal,

And records spun at the speed of crazed wheels
Taking you somewhere far from yourself,

Stars in a thin glitter, burnt out above
A swagger of smoke in the parking lot,

And then the Sunday bells and church doors open
To the half dead and the bed wetters,

Past the end of Genesis and deep into Deuteronomy,
Black book from which no one escaped,

Wound where the scruples put down roots,
Years before the fallen protocols and the undertow,

Before the wrought-iron agonies, sudden ripples in the heart,
Cordage of veins and the ropy tendons,

Before the ice, wind-whetted, at the lip of the downspout,
And sirens scaring the air with a bloody scream,

Blockage of wrecks on a gravel road, plunge of fire
In the tapped-out flats built by sawtooth and stud nail,

Before the darkness drained over everything, except
The unforgiving light in the guilty room.

95% of Love Is Half of What You Want

And there you are, shaking your maracas
In a backless dress. And here I am,
Slash pockets and a center vent, cool
As that blue-cut zircon nesting in
The small white hollow of your throat.

Dust on the dance floor wheels and frets
Like the atoms of my appetite,
And I can feel the friction: heat
Sliding up through my shoes;
Sizzle of silk from your seesaw hips.

Light drifts around us like the grain
Of old photographs, and we pose
In a slow pivot and swoop,
Acrobats of the loose erotic,
Revels in the blind unraveling.

Death makes it all more desperate,
More sweet: the density of flesh
Weakened by desire, giving way
To the plunge and flow, welcoming
Whatever comes to the wet thresholds.

My muse goes naked to the bone
And takes her vinegar straight.
But you want the soul of roses,
Marrow of the mind, beyond these
Crude codes of dirt and darkness.

And you tell me: Fool,
Forget the guzzle and the bungalows,
The mad reversion to the mean;
I don't believe in numbers over two
Or zero at the breaking point.

And so we spin, like straw into gold,
Smoothing our steps past

Blister and gristle: me with a tongue
Cured in black smoke, and you cresting
At the pleasure of the moon.

Moon Amour

Pale sister of the sun, veiled
In a hand-me-down light, don't believe
Everything you hear about
The sultry attraction of blondes. In your own
Elusive way, your cool beauty
Keeps coming back, younger again,
Glow to vanish to glow.
Faithful and inconstant girl, you float
On the dark above me, as if love
Weighed nothing at all, though each night
It drags my heart down
From heaven to the heavy earth.

Hermetically Sealed

Stanza, little room in which
I've locked the door
And drawn the heavy drapes,

Let's keep the lamplight low, the fan
Turned up so high
My mind won't weaken in the heat.

In this dry air, the words stay
Calm and tight,
The syntax closing in, cool to the touch.

I've seen too many poems
Spoiled by a loose line, a damp eye,
The creepy breathing of hysteria; I've heard

Pale ellipses longing for
The steel-toed boot,
Subjunctives cringing for the whip.

There's something to be said
For leather and wet silk, or the bijou
Theories of the Eurotrash,

But not here,
Where good things come in threes.
Stanza, my last stand,

Small cell in which
The strict laws of the letter
Set the spirit free,

Like a heart speeding its beat
Against the bony spokes,
I know my place.

Somewhere between
The soft bed and the hard
Rock on the radio,

I put my native tongue
To work, open to
The dark instincts of ecstasy.

Homage to John Ashbery

It's not as if the clouds, fast as they are, are getting better every year.
The winds still blow whereso'er they list,
And the jackrabbit don't mean jacksquat in the grand scheme of things.

In the grand scheme of things, somebody's always going to be left
To clean up the trash of catastrophes.
But that's not our problem: we have no plans to survive the final trump.

To survive the final trump, you've got to be holding at least five aces.
And it's not true that clean hands leave no fingerprints,
Or that the soul is spotless at birth, as everyone believes but no one
    knows.

Everyone believes but no one knows: where would religions be without
    our ignorance?
Here's your god, and here's their god,
And here's the door-to-door salesman, making do with sore feet and
    faith in himself—

Faith in himself, because he's learned how cranky this vacuum cleaner
    can be.
The housewife in her housecoat, curlers
Pink as a pig's prick, lets the big machine suck up whatever dirt's down
    there.

Whatever dirt's down there, it's not as if the clouds are any better, just
Hairballs, dust bunnies of the upper atmosphere,
And the wind sweeping them all away, leaving the heavens (my God!)
    godless and clean.

The Sexual, as Opposed to What

Stuck up there
On the tall screen, Minnie would
Mince around in those shoes
The size of cattle boats, a klutz,
But fetching, somehow;
Somehow, it was the heels, the teetery heels,
That brought her back to earth
And lifted her to a different level—

That, and the little mouse cunt
We must have known was there,
If only by the look on
Mickey's face, eyes stricken with awe,
Enormous on that bony rodent,
That animal in pants.

It made his ears twitch
In sublimation of the lower self,
As if to say: I'm a sweet guy
With a high voice, but
Deep in my blood
Another pulse peals through me, too.

Of course, it's all a cartoon: what isn't?
A flicker of light goes down
From eyeball to groin, and back again,
Picking its way through the dark,
As the lips squeak against themselves,
Red and swollen, below the hand
That paints them in, the animating hand,
Slower with every stroke.

Unrequited Dialogue by Moonlight

You don't have to believe in
Moonlight with its forgeries of frost, its crystals
Dripping down the windowpane. But why not
Believe in lies, if the world lies
Under a spell the truth can't break, too weak
For the white magic of the moon, for the black arts
Practiced by tobacco ads and presidents,
By Mistress Larissa with her boots and whips?

I'm not a moonshine kind of guy myself,
Though I've driven a dark highway
Listening to love songs soak up
Dead air from the radio and a stale Dodge.
If I turned the decibels down, maybe I could
Hear you better, all your arguments against
The placebo effect of April, the shade-tree philosophers,
An empire decked out like a blind mule
In spandex and rhinestones.

Would you say that even the false messiahs
Can pass a lie detector test? Would you say
It's belief that puts the bullets in the gun?
And I'd like to ask you why
Fanatics at the barricades brace up their faith
On blood like mother's milk, when more than ever
All I want is a dry martini so tall I'd have to
Stand on tiptoe to sip it, with an olive
Big as a pod from *The Body Snatchers*.

I'd like a few answers that would
Make the missionaries trade in their Bibles
For a jukebox and a sharkskin suit; that would
Convince me to walk this earth
In the only serious position, on all fours,
Like a hound sniffing out the backside of paradise.

I'd like to get a little testy and felonious—
But far off, in your time zone, it's
Always half past silence,
And that's way too late to call.

Amo, Amas, Amat

Those of you who know, and have always known,
Tragic possibilities in a soft hand, in hair
That tangles at some seductive touch,

May gather at midnight for the rites of love
And other punishments the stars pronounce,
Pillows white as moons from which you've weaned yourself,

Still mouthing desire with voluptuous tongues
That can no longer tell guilt from gratitude.
In the darker tawdry of your talk,

Where all verbs conjugate at the first person,
Your pallor comes from polishing the apple
Of the *I*: I saw, I took, I ate.

Corrosions of ammonia could do no worse,
Or theories of therapy, or solo flights,
Those secret sweet ascensions in the bed.

In the leopard's hide, the leopard feels at home.
But you are naked, a raw voice, a vapor,
The hiss of yes at the tail end of day,

Vermilion on the verge of indigo, the sky
Sliding past the wet light you were born to,
Brine and blood beyond the broken mother.

And what way back to the Palace of Pure Affection,
Hidden in Beijing, in the old Forbidden City?
The gates of China close against you still.

The ribs of the firecrib are black with ash.
The flames rise and crest like fever. And who
Hasn't felt the afterburn of love?

The heart mills, and the loins grind, and the lips
Kiss you to a calm, to a silent partner
With no control, no purpose but to pay—

The immensities of mind made small, the body
Its own Babylon, a human sacrifice
On the high altars of the lower gods.

Getting It Straight

What we have here is
A tree with a serious lean. And no wonder—
In this high wind,
Even the sky's not safe:
The mare's tails keep flicking the eagles away.

Over here, the bleeding heart
And baby's breath; over there, the birch
Like a scroll of old parchment
On which some hand has
Spelled out the black strokes of a poem.

I remember the early dusk,
The early fall, when all the leaves turned up
Their lifelines in the breeze.
It was a time for
Crystal pears and cool wines from Austria.

Those of us who still
Write letters, leaf after leaf, have learned
The erotics of absence,
Mind and body
Stripped down to bare words on a page.

But that was back in
The season of suffrage, when what counted was
Talk of cuts and economy.
These are the days of rogation,
Before the big lift and the rising sap.

Still, the birch can't seem
To get it straight, not like the catalpa tree
With its green linga,
Seed pods in a droop,
Or the samaras of maple taking a dive.

And the bees are out, too,
Not in the off-white hives of blossom
On the buckeye, but in
The backyard at every petal,
A scrum hunched in their rugby brown and gold—

The backyard, where
Squirrels slide off the glass of the finch feeder,
And all the yellow afternoon
Sparrows roll in the dust,
Too lazy to scratch a living from the front lawn.

The whole planet's
Stricken by the ugly buzz of being born.
I'm still waiting for
Another annunciation,
Some complicated air for virginal by Byrd.

Meanwhile, the day
Bends downward, and each tree, from the pine
To the star magnolia,
Foreshadows the dark,
Lies longer than itself as the sun gives up.

On a night like now,
Anything even half alive, alow or aloft,
Could use a drink. I toast
The marshmallow moon
And slip a little whiskey to the potted plant.

Spoils

Redeyed at night, the coon and possum
Bristle through the backyards, hunched ahead
Like small shrubs on the move, a slow hairy
Landscape that bares its teeth at trash and trouble.

So many enemies under a dangerous spray of moon:
Dogs on the growl, the speed of wheels, all those
Slippery sides that go down deep and trap them,
Desire scrabbling at the bottom of the dark.

Faithful to hunger, they nose out what they need,
Dirty leavings that still reek from the body's
Urge for salt, for grease, for every mess
We make and crave and can't keep the lid on.

Downloading the Meltdown

Rumple of clouds at sunset, low and pink,
Underbelly of heaven in the summer slack, and me

Depressed as a backdoor detective on a case of slow clues.
I'm never lonely as long as I have my own body

To interrogate, my mind with its whips and pincers.
I buckle at the slightest threat; I confess

In the high pure pang of a choirboy singing
At some ceremonious occasion for the faint of heart.

And now the hot night, the moon cool as a bishop
In a boudoir. What you can't get over,

You must get past. Through a haze of smoke and rum,
What's left of me squints at the odds and ends.

Profile in a Shadow Box

I muck my mind out twice a day
And lay down
Sweet straw for an afternoon nap,
For the night's long skid toward oblivion,

Where I breathe deep the chloroform of dreams
Until I'm sky-eyed
And soul-loose, rapscallion walking
The lines of least resistance,

Awkward and lucky,
Like a man with three balls, and grateful not to be
Assistant manager of a Taco Bell
Or rat wrangler for a cancer lab.

⊚ ⊚ ⊚

When I hear the heel of sleet
Against a car roof, or see it glaze the trees
Until they drop
Like stunned cattle in a chute,

I know winter still bends the world its way,
Under the stitch
And masonry of snow, with a wind
That chills the ear like chrome harmonicas.

And what can I do but wait
Until the sun
Beats down like a tambourine
And rattles the daffodils out of mud?

I want the spark of dogwood petals
And cattails tipped
By a scold of crows. I want to live on nothing
But succotash and hogs roasted in a slow smoke.

⊚ ⊚ ⊚

At the hour of pleasant melancholy,
The hour when I serve myself from the bottle,
Bartender and barfly,
I wrap my hand, tortoise skin baggy at the knuckles,

Around a glass of something vile enough
To silence jubilees.
Let the moon tonight come up subdued,
A moon of potholes and ghostly powder,

A moon too dark for suicides
To sharpen their blades or tighten a sliding noose—
And the stars
Like little bells too high for hearing.

    ◎ ◎ ◎

Wakes and weddings. The dead and condemned.
Ah, the dead
In their dependable plenitude, always so sober
After the arteries collapse and the gut goes south.

And on top of the cake, those sweet effigies of
Bride and groom,
Feet stuck in the icing, before the big knife
Slices all apart, his hand guiding hers.

I'll never get used to the lamentations
And the singsong vows, hard rice
Falling from heaven on the innocent, and dirt rising
Around the box.

    ◎ ◎ ◎

I admire the lightbulb turned on all night,
Like the head of an infant prodigy,
So much joy
Pushing the dark away.

When I burn out, you can ship my scorched soul,
Packed deep in excelsior and the green
Leaves of summersweet,
Back to the faulty manufacturer.

◉ ◉ ◉

I'm at loose ends in the rainlight,
My mind somewhere else, always dawdling
Through the sprawl,
In this insolent America of steel and fact.

Grackles hunch on a power line, black as priests
Hatching a plot,
And robins writhe like Holy Rollers,
Ecstatic in the spring pools.

Is this first frail blossom
Revenge on so much snow? I'm not sure
How anything can be both
Naked and secret.

And then the sun comes in a panic of elation,
Making me happy once more
To fall into
Love and its infinite mistakes.

Not Dead but Deading

Indian summer, a buttery sun over the drifting leaves,
On a day made for cloudberry jam and ceremonies of the teapot.

But I've spent all morning on this messy sheet, my own words
Strangled by my own hand. I might as well have cruised

The ethernet, mousing down a site for cold volcanoes. Outside,
Light shifts on the birch bark, opening a window in the tree.

A spider's sticky silk shimmers under the footfall of a fly.
What was I thinking? I wasn't thinking anything. The body

Runs itself, cranky apparatus of outspouts and intake valves.
I could use some woofers in the wayback, to make the eyeballs jump.

The season's not dead but deading, no more than a spark
Flared up in false fire, like a souvenir of some private pleasure,

Seashells or dog collar or tickets to the last concert of the Doors.
And a sorrowful gospel don't bring the bacon home.

If I must be reborn, make it another vaginal delivery.
And let my mind find its balance like a squirrel on a power line.

There's no unified theory of the heart, only friction and flesh
And fluent apologies, with a little backtalk on the side.

So October's easing its way to the mineral months, raising
Gusts of confetti from the maple, late elation from the raw-boned oak.

Exhaustion

I lie down in the Dark Ages, another night deficient in ecstasy.

I'm tired of the old laws and the new laws and the laws they've been
thinking up between breakfast and delirium.

I might as well be driving a dogsled in the white waste of Alaska, mukluks
still feral on my feet,

Or sliding a two-ton truck through Alabama mud, a seizure of fiddles on
the radio and a bumper sticker that says: *Living in a vacuum sucks.*

The world's run short of taffeta and courtesy and grass widows with a
gamy scent.

And where are you, bare spark at the flash point, when I need the moony
spasms of release?

I'm tired of all the stagestruck mothers with little Hamlets in the womb,
and those snake handlers whipping Jesus in the lead with their rattlers
and cottonmouths.

And I'm worn out from the terror, the gruesome excuses for a heart
packed in dry ice and a flag strung up by the neck.

The heart frightens me, too, the way it motors off on its own, with no
backup, no redundant systems for the pump.

So what's the weather like in the otherworld? Same today as the last
eternity—nothing changes where everything's changed.

Even the Bible's been divided into tongues, from the Aramaic all the way
to gangster slang: *So they brung him down the cross, and the guy's already colder
than a Jersey whore.*

And what about you? Idle hands, when I could use another volunteer to
stir the fleshpots.

I've survived the drumrolls and the German sense of humor and the
bloody flux—why isn't it someone else's turn to pull the temple down?

I'm not feeling world historical tonight, though I can still smell the stench
of a rotten hypothesis, like eggheads left out too long in the sun.

My mind's one wrinkle away from ravenous black—spiders in the brainpan,
and all circuits down on the motherboard.

And I'm so tired of death shouldering his scythe across the fields,
grasshoppers leaping from his bony toes.

Give me freshets from the belly; quicken my desire by some strange order
of magnitude; fix me a poultice to bring the swelling down.

The hour already feels tainted and ancient. And then, at the low stroke of
the soul, you come.

Solving for the Unknown

Winter's waving its white flag, but I'm the one who surrenders,
The days still so wrapped in snow there's no hope for
Siberian squill, small and fresh and blue-faced, rising from bulbs
Whose inner scales, dried and set out in a dark corner, could kill a rat.

These nights, I feel low down as a stump with a bullfrog on top,
Bad dreams, and a hard-on scuffing the sheets: all those grain-fed girls
From the flatlands, pierced ears and painted nails, squiggly in their jeans,
Every crease and crevice making my cowlick quiver like an ant's
    antenna.

Civilian in the God wars, unchurched and uncomplaining, I don't mind
Sundays devoted to roasts and gooseberry fool, and Wednesdays
Free from novenas of sore knees, Latin gone dead in the mouth again,
Given over to a false vernacular, the hymns less lofty than before.

My music flares up like a factory stack: kick drum and a dry snare,
Red Garland driving the piano, pedal down and a broken road ahead.
It tells me there's always a lug nut loose on the wheel. It tells me,
In stop-time and blue note, the wisest word in the language is *No*.

All my flyblown ancestors from Sicily kept their lips shut,
Omerta the motto of the tribe. And I've tied up my tongue, too,
In a lover's knot. But the heart won't stay quiet, won't quit:
Its trapdoors open like blossoms in the late bloodrush of spring.

Mythos of Honey and Brine

Elegance of your hands around me;
Fresh fruit of your mouth on mine;
Love welling up from a deep wound—

Loosen your throat and tell me,
Flesh dense with desire, how once
You were Europa mounted by a bull,

Bellow of the sea swell and horns heaving,
The white bull Zeus who opened you
To secret ecstasies of god and beast.

⊙ **TWO**

You don't learn the cancan at obedience school.
—JOHN ASHBERY

Category Error

You won't find me among the drones in a drawing room
Or Bible to Bible with the pious in their beeswax pews.

I'm far too busy scraping rust off the ironies and soaking them deep
In my own brine and vinegar. Should I embrace the bores

And bless the true believers, whatever they might believe in—
Carrot juice or bazookas or Jesus of the desolate flesh?

Should I suffer for something I haven't done, even if I weaseled away
From so much else on the sly? I'm buying no pancakes for the hangman.

Won't somebody bring me a strong and righteous drink? For I am dry
Down to the spleen, sober and tired and prone to promiscuous fits

Against the weather and the government, when only liquor will lift me
Out of this wreckage into that heathen eloquence the world deserves.

I'd like a little barnyard guitar and a woman tall in vertiginous heels,
Her tongue sautéed in her own hot saliva, and everything unzipped.

You can have all those lessons on the incorruptible, all that
Star stuff high in the woozy heavens. I'm not done with the dirt.

Getting Down with the Mofos

Squawk, squawk. Why wear a beard and beret,
And polish the pear-shaped vowels, the granite consonants?

However much the songbirds mean to you,
You can't spend your whole life drowning cats.

I'll take some flint with my flannel, some honey
Among the hisses and the glottal stops.

On the bus, half the earphones clatter with rap,
Like a drill bit to the grieving brain.

I'll take some candles and brandy with my crude stew,
A little whiff of critter behind the jasmine.

Toad, old croak fat with flies, you know
The quick and sticky tongue brings the dinner in.

Prayer from the Back Pew

God of pain, God of the crazy idolaters,
Father of ash and the spiny virtues,
I'm not like that good thief
Sucking up to Jesus on a long afternoon
When the sun burned through everything
But blood and judgment. Maybe
I'm enrolled in the wrong religion.
Not everyone wants to be redeemed
Like a wedding ring from a pawnshop.
And it's hard for me to reconcile
Those two testaments, the old one remote
As silent film, the new one close up,
As if a shaky camera had been strapped
To the chest of each disciple.
But I'm not eager to believe anything
So strange you must be born to it:
Greek gods run amuck in the mountains
Or heathen spirits from the hot countries—
Too many extra arms, and the creepy heads
Of bird and beast. I'm looking for
A faith that won't torch the body
With its own desire, or make the mind
Crawl back inside its bony shell.
What good is good, if it leaves
Innocence at the mercy of itself,
Or strands us in some lesser heaven
Below the vain angels and high priests?
And hell's no better: I almost
Pity Satan, stuck down there for eternity
With all those losers underfoot.
Deliver me into a cooler credence
Of my own. I could croon hosannas
To a Roman gorgeousness of gold,
A Quaker silence in the heart,
And nineteen virgins fanning me
In some oasis of the afterworld.
I could write a gospel of the earth

Untamed and succulent. Let's start
With a garden and end with a garden,
No fruits forbidden, and no savior
Dead to spring me from this dust—
Only the savor of each sweet day.
Let's live in paradox and never fall
For any truth more naked than ourselves.

No, and I Wouldn't Name My Cat Cleopatra, Either

I like the lonely, one-eyed look
Of the period: it tells
The tired sentence when to stop.
(Parentheses travel in pairs,
Chaperones of the stray thought.)

I like Sodom, but not Gomorrah—
Though I could change my choice
If some scholar of the sand dug up
A second salty sin from the twin cities.

I like the South and all its syllables,
Slow as honey in the mouth
And sweeter than your Yankee tongue.

Of all the bears, I like the grizzly best,
As big as God and twice as hairy.

My favorite music? The hum of an idle mind.

While I have nothing against the sun,
I love the sound of *parasol.*

When it comes to sleep, I like
Nude naps in the afternoon
More than the dry dreams of insomnia.

From food in all its forms, I prefer
Tomatoes mated with olive oil—
In sauces, in salads, or on the side,
And over the vast wetlands of spaghetti.

And when I die, I'd like cremation,
Not some somber burial; and in memory of my ashes,
A service of Elvis impersonators, old and fat,
And flowers in tall vases on the crates of booze,
And for my wife, the cold cash of combat pay.

Idling through Rinehart's Brain

Over here, the permalust, depravities on the mattress,
And over there, the highest notes of woe.

He might be wondering what's for dinner tonight,
Coquille St. Jacque or Kool-Aid and fish sticks.

He might be sighing for Paris, those cheroots and arias,
A little nap inside the sleeve of afternoon.

For all we know, there's light strangled in every cranny,
Gossip and rumination in the lower lobes.

For all we know, he's thinking: My hair may be
Backing up, but my mind's going forward.

So many stretch marks and erosions, so many ideas
Fizzling in the fault lines like a nimbus of gnats!

Group Therapy for the Bards

We all sat in a circle, leaning in
On the kinds of chairs you might find
Unfolded for a meeting of the PTA,
Like angry parents planning their assault
On satanic rituals in *The Night before Christmas*
And the blue-eyed hegemony of algebra.

We were making the dirt fly, digging deep
Inside the buried sources of our shame
And failure, down to the mutilated roots,
Boy bards and graybeards weeping for all
Those hours lost in the milky tinct of laudanum
Or in the wrinkled valleys of the brown rose.

In this kinship of the sick and saved,
What couldn't we confess? Some still bent low
To a god who gave us winter and the twin bed,
And the disciplines of stick and stone; and some
Warmed up an April of inducements, a May of misrule,
Everlasting permissions of the windfall flesh.

Even the prim women let down their locks,
Buns and braids unloosed in a millrace
Or the writhing spikes of Medusa. No more
Sonnets marked with an X chromosome,
Or music like the ornamental bark of a lap dog;
No more bread and butter notes to the muse.

And even the strict constructionists agreed
There's more than one way to scan a poem.
Victims of the foot fetish now felt close
To those out of step with the drum-and-brassbound
Parade of pentameters, and nearer yet to those
Who measured out their lines with cocaine spoons.

The ancients held fast to their complaints,
Tired of signing on as front men for the emperor
Or ghostwriters for an oracle, tired of spinning out

Those action tales around the raw light of a campfire,
As if violence improvised at a steady stroke
Could move the world away from wrath and madness.

Only the troubadours, with their inlaid lutes and loves,
Sang sweetly among the weasels and the ingenues,
Picking a tune through the suicides, the silence
Of mouths pried open by a tongue depressor,
Through gunrunners and gossips, informers for the art police,
And nervous amateurs out to copyright their dreams.

In that chorus of sandpaper and kazoos, so many
Moaned about their early poems: the stillborn or aborted;
The infants streaked with talcum, too tender yet to feel
Desire swelling the belly, man hair matting the jaw;
The baby bastards in the snow, abandoned to the cold
Barrens of a page, where voices winced on every word.

Beyond the tricks of expectation, the easy probings of repair,
We talked out all the lies and pride, mining the bitter mysteries
For what remained: eclipse of clinkers on a slag heap,
Or rough stones brought up from the dark, a havoc of adamants
That might, if beveled on the right bias, become
A blue erudition of diamonds in the jeweler's hand.

Dating Cassandra

And what to give a girl
Who knows everything? Not that I believe her—
The penknives and cruelties, outtakes
From the shaky frames of disaster, loners
Morose in the shrubbery—
But even the tea leaves are turning
Autumnal shades. And there's no place for dry wit
When you're drowning.

Sometimes I take her, in the afternoons,
To the Maison Amnesia, and put her through
Those rare positions only the wicked know—
The Salamander and the Butter Churn.
On a scale of mud to moon,
She barely rises
To the high-strung trembling of the power lines.

And you have to love it because
That's all there is to love. I can't keep her
From the sick streets,
Decoding the mimes or spooking
The rubes in their dewlaps, like a shark
Teaching the tourists a little discipline.
And what do they learn? Nothing but
The spiky urge of appetite.

Secrets insist on being known, even down
To quicklime and a fast prayer.
But I'm no critic: I don't live
For the creepy pleasures of the postmortem.
So you can stuff another
Sock in the wisecrack: she's not out there
Glad-handing the refugees or singing
That starstruck anthem like
The last chorus of "Heartbreak Hotel."

To the spoiled go the spoils.
In the vast American twilight, in the cornfields

Left to the rats and the rattling wind,
Ruthless and innocent, where loosestrife
Leans exhausted on the air, what
Can she do, over and over,
But tell you
The uncontrollable truth?

Petitions to the Tenderloin

Sisters of the wet sleeve and the warm abyss,
Why don't you teach me
The Persian possibilities of love?

I can count on you, muses of the dark libido,
To know some tricks they never whispered of between
The stiff sheets at convent school.

From your own reckless lips, let me hear
The tales of fur and succulence, tremblings at a touch
Before the great racy plunge.

You can't spend all your time seducing the newsboys,
Or buttering virgins in the mezzanine, or other
Matinee amusements too amorous to name.

I need instructions as much as the bishop's niece
And more than any student of the acrobatic books.
Apprentice me to mysteries of the flesh.

You were there when Venus stepped ashore
From her oyster shell, still salty
As split herrings on a breakfast plate.

And you cleaned up on the towel concession
In the Cities of the Plain,
Backdoor profits before the fires fell.

Who can sleep on these puritan pillows
Or watch the wallpaper close in,
Tight stripes like the bars of a prison cell?

Daughters of indulgence, I might as well be
Some lame Ukrainian with a glass eye, strangling
On the drawstrings of my tame pajamas.

I want to know about the half lotus and the bullwhip,
The milkman swagger and the honeymoon tattoos.
Make my hair stand up like a five-inch heel.

It's not too late to sow the old garden with
Dame's rocket and goatsbeard, and free
The mossy perfumed springs of gin on the rocks.

You can lock the gates behind you and leave me there,
Writhing my tongue like a green snake,
Jade in the jaded grass.

Midnight at the *Club Imaginaire*

It's like this: I'm sitting in the sacramental dark of a nightclub,
At a small round table sometime in the early Thirties, when the world
Paid for its gin a bullet a bottle, and the hatcheck girl and the cigarette girl
Both looked like second leads in a film of shadows and machine guns,
Hair swept up in a golden roll, faces smiling on empty, smart enough to know
It wasn't their brains that brought them this job, but the loose lilt
Of their breasts and the tight lines below. A small round rump
Bumps by me down the pinball lanes, a drummer's ricochet among the tables
Crowded close to the bandstand, the singer posing pale and cool
Against the pink pavilion of a scallop shell, torch songs in a sconce,
Blue sequins steaming from her throaty moan in some stillbirth of the blues.

What am I doing here? I haven't been born yet, and already I know
How to smoke, how to order martinis straight up, at the bottom a twist
Or an olive with a bloodshot eye. No monkey rum for me, no bourbon
Drained from a bathtub or dripped down the copper tubing to a Mason jar.
Across the black lacquer, dyslexic link of rings in some Olympics for the
   weird,
I'm writing my gnome notes on a napkin, cryptics of ink in a wet spread—
Gangster haiku ahead of its time, with a big bass beat like a hard salami
On the back of the neck, tiny odes to all those millions off the books,
And those mob guys in their dark fedoras, tilted low at the brim, and their
   slick suits,
Chalk stripes as if the body were its own worst prophet and could see
Sketched on the sidewalk an outline of assassinated limbs.

You've come because you love the underlife, citizens of the shovel and the
   landfill,
Bubbles of blood rising from the hurt waters of the harbor. You've left
   behind
Your mother with her soapy pieties, prayers in a hairshirt, prepared to meet
   her God,
And your father buried in his briefcase beneath the pickled lawns of
   suburbia.
I've come to love your hands trembling around the misfire of a matchstick,
The twitch of excitable lips, and the red tongue that lights your laughter.
What can I lose? In this spill of dream, this whim of white diamonds

Laced above your collarbones, and the cling of quicksilver you move so
    easily in,
I'll take the risk of taking you, a bad bargain of damaged goods. We'll drift
Among the dancers, that slow fuse of beauty and the brute, and keep time
Where it belongs: beyond the reach of midnight and the slippery laws of
    sleep.

Mad in Manhattan

Oh, to have lived in New York, in some coldwater dump,
Mad for art in the days of Man Ray and Duchamp
And the Baroness Elsa von Freytag-Loringhoven!

To have walked the trashy and elegant streets, to the studio
Of the wild Picabia, and stared at his *Shining Vagina*
And the Baroness Elsa von Freytag-Loringhoven!

To go slumming among the poets and the heroes of paint, to have
Swooned at the feet of the avant-garde and the derriere
Of the Baroness Elsa von Freytag-Loringhoven!

To have seen the cancelled stamps on her face and the soup can bra,
Coal scoop for a hat and bustle with a taillight, all worn
By the Baroness Elsa von Freytag-Loringhoven!

I was born for an age of mystery and genius and junk, not these years
Of the frozen soul, but the reckless gaze, the crazy heart,
And the Baroness Elsa von Freytag-Loringhoven!

Fabulous, Just Fabulous

In my own Eden, I'd have the plants and animals
Painted as if they stepped
Fresh from the oily panel of a canvas—
Leopards by Pollock, baboons by Francis Bacon,
And the creamy roses from Renoir's hand.

◎ ◎ ◎

In the swollen story of our kind, what mutants
Had to mate, somewhere
Between the sabertooth and the cell phone,
To seed me here: Caliban with a banjo and a bitter grunt,
And no opinion on the postcolonial love poem?

◎ ◎ ◎

Does the Grand Scheme of Things imply behind it
A Grand Schemer? If so,
I'd like to sue that sorry tease for
Negligence and breach of contract, my case taken up by
The bow-tied shysters at Malice, Underhand, and Glee.

◎ ◎ ◎

In some lost ancient life, I might have been
A baby in Babylon
Or a spokesman for the burning wheel.
But the years come down to this: Time, with its clubfoot,
Dragging my slow days through the dirt.

◎ ◎ ◎

I can no longer tell the difference between
Sublime and slime, or
Raise the gate that keeps the low pleasures
From flowing through. How can nothing feel so heavy,
Like the hole in the middle of a millstone?

◎ ◎ ◎

In my own *Divine Comedy*, I'd give the afterlife
More laughs, less God.
I'd put an elevator in, from the bottomlands
To a station beyond the stars, so cold and black no one
Would leave the hard-burnt suburbs of hell.

◎ ◎ ◎

What year, in my dream of peace, lies untroubled,
Arcadia of the safe?
What red-letter day stays dry and quiet
On the calendar of blood? Even the hour of my birth
Keeps receding, as far away as my mother's pain.

◎ ◎ ◎

The two-pack hack, the cough of forty years, wheeze
From the spongy lungs—
I join the outcast congregation of tobacco,
Breathless in the gales of May or the rogue snows of October,
Lighting our candles to the Lord of Smoke.

◎ ◎ ◎

I'd like to believe in a heaven of love, and yet
Jesus sends me
No valentines, and no saints downsize a halo
For a friendship ring. I might as well place my faith in
A dog that licks me up from toes to nose.

◎ ◎ ◎

I've put a lot of mileage on the alphabet,
Taking shortcuts
To the long view, freewheeling down the dark,
And where has it got me? Skid marks on every page, words
Surging as they slip, here and here and here.

⊚ ⊚ ⊚

Do I suffer the first signs of incremental stupidity?
Or has the world become
Some late-onset Paris of the impossible,
Where I stall in the foreign streets like a tourist
With a map of downtown Dubuque?

⊚ ⊚ ⊚

In my own *Hamlet*, I'd play the upstage prince.
Dead father, mother
In a rut, kingdom gone wild around me—
I'd tame it all with a flameproof tongue, and stir
The shy fires of Ophelia twice a night.

⊚ ⊚ ⊚

My state of sulfur and salt and sugar cane,
I'm so tired of
Inconvenient ancestors and pregnant ghosts.
Once I could recite the principal exports from Euphoria,
And now my name's among them.

Pitching Woo

You want a man who's not all
Gollies and galoshes,
The head-rattling reek of cowcakes in a spring field.

Nor could you love
Some little dude too fond of doodads,
Wisp of nostalgia curling from his Bozo hair.

It's me you crave, baby, even if
You don't know it yet,
Blackout in the crystal ball of your noggin.

You won't find me
In a three-piece suit and a silver bracelet,
Portfolios under my pinstriped arm.

You won't catch me at the coon hunt
Or the tractor pull,
Biceps rising like an Alabama moon.

But when my voice
Slides over you, you'll feel
Something breaking in your jackhammer heart.

And when my eyes, sleek as
Two stallions in the sweat-stained night,
Darken as yours do,

How could you resist?
From the cold ceremony of the stars
Comes such heat

We'll burn below
And bark like dogs in the dog days. And after that,
The less said, the better.

Homage to Mr. Bones

> Goodbye, sir, & fare well. You're in the clear.
> —JOHN BERRYMAN

The amorous cat and the dog with three barks,
Woof woof woof, lounge around you in the backyard:
Not all days are ornery.
It's not my home, but I could picnic there:
Burgers on the grill, the dizzy roses, dead friends and ex-wives
Chatting up the children and the pets.

Better, in every way, than downtown with the young gods,
Designer beers in designer bars, and sea-salt pretzels
Half the size of snowshoes,
The women dazzling and gone, leaving little mysteries behind
Like their scent, like napkins crushed with their lipstick,
Empty mouths littering the tabletops.

You were, sir, the minstrel master of the neighborhood,
At ease among the high particulars and the baby talk,
Syntax astray, and midnights
Crazy with grief and booze. You left behind no goodbye
But your books, the words still floating somewhere
Between the river and the bridge.

Propertius at the Moonlight Lounge and Patio

The waitress brings my third martini out on a shaky tray,
Blonde curl of lemon in the silver gin. Halfway through October,
And already the air's so cool it pops her nipples up
Like the little gadget on a turkey breast that tells you
It's Thanksgiving, folks, time to gorge yourselves on gratitude.

And for what should I feel grateful tonight? The paper lanterns
Swell over me like stars on steroids, pale pinks and creams.
Everywhere I look, the season's slipped from ripe to rot.

Even Cynthia, my angel of temptation from the darker side of heaven,
Now goes by Cindy, she who used to shower in her pearls.
What I get from her these days are cranky rants and cold kisses,
Dates broken an hour before they're due, a kind of buzzard love
That gnaws my heart, half dead from all the beatings it gives itself.

Lately, I hesitate in front of her. Should I let my hair down,
Or my pants? My life's a Miranda warning: Anything I say
May be used against me. Ah, Cindy, my abbreviated dear,
Lady of the wayward fables, dizzy mistress of my vertigo!

And why should I count on her consoling tongue for peace?
All over the world, harebrained angers outfox the diplomats.
History has its foot in the door and won't take no for an answer.
Over a bloat of disposable soldiers, cross and crescent
Duke it out in the bloody sand, where any fool would give up
His God for a mouthful of foul water. I wouldn't mind
An alien invasion from some stump of the universe beyond
The telescopes, ugly mugs with a bit of extra in the knowhow,
Enough to knock the wobbly axis of this planet back to balance.

Closer to home, I've had my share of greedy healers,
Bishops of the soft glove and the hard staff, and all those
Entrepreneurs of the pulpit in their grins and bespoke suits,
Conspiring with the pieties until I'm ready to baptize myself
In the Church of Exasperated Jesus, no money down, no guarantees.

On the Moonlight patio, dahlias tied to the tall stakes
Lean and sprawl and shake their spiky heads. I'm drinking

A new gin that smells of cucumber and rose petals, with an olive
Pierced through the gizzard by a plastic sword. And I know
How that feels: we're all martyrs to someone else's pleasure.

My Cindy, my rawboned darling, aloft in her skyscraper heels,
The sort of woman who could wear a rattlesnake as a necklace,
Always gives me fresh reasons to be hurt, as if a queen
Had made me Grand Panjandrum in the Order of the Hindmost.

But I'm still not crippled by some telethon disease, and every dream
Is not a worst case scenario. I haven't been run to ground
By the bluenose bloodhounds of empire, or been appointed
Asshole in charge of patriotic felonies on the sly Potomac. My lines
Keep to themselves, civilians in the tribal snarl, though they sing
Against the grain while the lights flicker and the sweat drips.

Oh Cindy, my Darwinian proof, I'm no better than my betters,
As coarse as pope jokes and Jew riddles at the corner bar.
I wish I could peel a word like a peach and let the juice
Sluice out as Casanova did, that devious Venetian sleek in love.

But this century's too full of insults and velocity, too many
Fidgets and collisions for a solo on the midriff, a riff on the soul.
Should I defer to the future, or take this rusty wreck of myself
To the Heart Repair Shop? They can clean the parts in alcohol
And put them back together with steel screws, and I'll still be
Neither freak nor hero, even if my blood runs the wrong way,
And my mind's fucked up, and I can't tell right from ruin.

Toast

It's one of those mornings when you
Feel you were born
In some little horsepiss town in Texas.

And when you step into
The pup tent of your pants, into shoes
Like dogsleds in a tangled trace,

Rigged up wrong to face the day, well, by then
You're sure there's something
Absent from your life, like Hitler's testicle,

And we all know what knives and ashes
Flashed from that angry arrogance,
That lopsided brain.

But you have your own
Dark priorities,
Residue of the single malt and the double-dome.

Dirty Ulysses, you're late again,
Unmastered by the sirens, barely more human
Than your brother swine—

You and all the other Mortimers out there
Who carry death like a beehive
Inside your wooden heads.

You'd better forget about
That greasy sun of run-down egg, that sausage
Like the missing link.

Take this glass of milk that must have come
From cows gone sour on the hoof,
And this flaming toast you've already forked up.

It's one of those mornings when
Nothing will let you find
A shaky balance between needs and grief.

Coupling on the Edge of Entropy

And here I am again, carrying water for the damned,
When I should be riding out to neon nightclubs

In the back of a limousine, a car so big it flattens cats
And takes tight corners like a problem in geometry,

With a license plate that reads *Free Verse or Die*
And ten speakers shaken by Big Mabel and the Ballbreakers.

Hiding from heaven, where the dark haloes flash on
Like crime lights when you step in the wrong direction,

Where all the angels train with the IRS, I still believe
In the mercy of earth, in pardons retroactive to the womb.

Let bygones be herecomes, and the last supper served up
As lazy plates of meatloaf and tall bottles of Bud.

But even then, what utopia would not collapse
Under its own happiness? Ah, my friend, wintering down there

In Pinesap, Mississippi, like a rabbit in the sweet weeds,
You've never been struck by lightning, but often by

Hailstones thrown down as if God, after all,
Did play at dice, and loaded them to make His number.

I've seen those snake eyes, too, a glare in the dim garden,
Like two figs at the bottom of the fig leaf.

There may be nothing new under the sun, but something stirs
Below the sick moon pale from pulling tides all night.

I've heard the groan of continents that grind against each other
For the last inch of lebensraum in the sucking dirt.

Even if I could live like a prophet on grasshoppers and dew,
Shouting out my bearded visions to the birds

Until the sky caved in, stars under my feet like spent gravel,
What's one man against the laws of a raucous universe?

From that stammer and crack, that inbred wail, I'll take
The echo's ring and marry my own shadow, my bitter half.

Variations without a Theme

1. In the wreckage of the heart, somebody has always run the stop sign.

2. There's a theory for everything, but not a Theory of Everything, not one proven down to the last decimal point, one that would satisfy the lost explorers striking their little waxy matches deep in the cave.

3. Near sunset, the clouds heap up like the blushing buttocks of Greek goddesses. At such times, I wish that heaven were not beyond my reach.

4. I can think of several people who might want to kill me, but not one is Muslim.

5. Sometimes I'm torn between guilt and ease, as if work alone would set me free, as if sitting here, my mind at idle, were not its own kind of slow and sweatless labor.

6. North and south, a few have struggled in cold glory to reach the poles. But there's a good reason you won't find a balcony on an igloo.

7. I'm far too old for the low life—decadence at a distance is all I'm game for, and a quick piss at three a.m.

8. Summer's at an end, and it's all over—tomatoes, the ballpark, fireflies like little lighthouses washed out to sea. And now the schooling, now the early dark.

9. *If it's not too much trouble*, some will say. But, of course, it's always too much trouble, when what I want is just enough trouble, just enough heartbreak and mayhem to get by.

⊙ THREE

And we are put on earth a little space.
That we may learn to bear the beams of love.
—WILLIAM BLAKE

À Contrecoeur

Sometimes I feel afraid for it, my heart
       like a mouse in a windmill,
             in an avalanche of grain.

Lay your face against my flesh and listen:
       first throb, then seep, then silence
             like the stifled cries from an orphanage.

Press your hand there, skin on skin, down
       where the cranky blood jerks through,
             dense and empty as the dark.

Or would you rather reach past bone to put
       your fist around that fist,
             and touch my heart at last?

Variations in Vertigo

I've been listening to the burr of a stand-up bass
Behind the brushes and the rolling arpeggios,
Jaunt of the keys going down on a catquick piano.

I've been thinking of birth and beyond,
And the reasons for love. Love has no reason,
And for that the moon spills more mercy than the mind.

I remember the boys in their white tee shirts, cuffs
Turned up on the dungarees, and the girls
Smoking menthol, cool to the root of their tongues.

Were those the years of goose flesh and hair of the dog,
Grasshopper hearts idling in the summer nights?
Or was I mistaken? I was mistaken, again and again.

I've been lost in the simmer of cymbals, in a one-legged bass
Sidesliding to the blues, in a drive of ivories
That justify the lines like a razor through cocaine.

I've been watching the day gain on the dark—
Fat shadows to noon of no shadow, then the long lean of shade,
Evening taking back the ground it gave to light.

Should I muse on the four rivers of paradise
Or another one, far from the garden, leaping off a cliff,
A suicide of water frothing all the wild way down?

I've been brooding over the fall of Orpheus,
With his lyre and his bad luck and a taste for women
Who ripped the songs out of his bloody head.

Is there a wishbone in the drumstick, an endnote
Plucked from the bottom of the bass?
I've been following the stride of crooked fingers

Across the grand, as if they walked a tightrope
Trembling under them, high
In the nervous certainty of the next step.

Private Conversations in Public Places

Shudder of a cell phone in the heart pocket,
Some signal from a distant town, or near to home,
Or from the darker precincts of the moon.

Who out there has my number?
Who knows enough to make me pause
In the rustling of palm trees and bougainvillea?

What the night sea murmurs, I have no answer for.
Is that you at the other end of the line,
Voice that calls me to myself, out of interrupted air?

It's not too late for me to listen,
Or to speak among the strangers who lean away,
My mouth warm against your ear.

Low Tide on the Sunset Coast

Cocktails when the sky turns
From ornery to ornament, that hour when
Seabirds swim against the sun and the clouds keep
Every color the air can take, citron going to gold, gold
Gone to coral and mauve and aquamarine,
Alcoholic Floridas of the ripened eye—

And she wants to feel herself
Inside the long swoon of a negligee
That clings like sweat, that pours down
The swollen slopes of desire,
A glycerin kiss of silk
Before it's lifted like a tide
Peeled back from the beach, the sand
Darker now in the damp shadows of evening—

And through the glass slats and screens
On the dim verandah, she sees
A rind of light along the shoreline
And stars like a broken bracelet of white shells.
Mangrove and palm and pine, and vines around them
Like veins on a brawny arm—why would she need
A stiff-necked rose or any colder bloom?
In the swampwood Keys of wicker and stucco,
At the end of rutroads that drown
Each night in the moonburnt sea, she gives herself
To the salt and sultry lusters of the Gulf.

Fantasia on a Phrase from Don DeLillo

Women in warm climates
smell of clove and white camellias,
their skin smooth as if
born from the lost wax process.

Susceptible to weather,
women in warm climates
drowse under the drugged light of sun,
and at the chill's least ripple
press themselves against
the windfall flame in the firecrib.

Women in warm climates
need no preface to pleasure, no blouse
transparent on the banked breasts.
Ambassadors from the moon,
the oils panting through them
in a quick rinse, they feel
the same pull and slur as the sea.

Women in warm climates
pause at the brink of stairways,
unwrinkling
the haze of lace, their brows
mapless in the tight light.

Unknown to science or the testaments,
women in warm climates
vibrate inside themselves an extra membrane,
like a pulse of wet plums.

Women in warm climates
keep a secret beat
for the strut of a brother, that cool stroke,
that little hitch and a glide.

Not silver, that desperate metal, nor gold
gussied up for kings and whores—

women in warm climates
wear no slink of slave chain at the wrist,
nothing on their necks
but the oval yoke of their own bone.

Women in warm climates
leave a kiss like a snail's trace,
slow and slick.

Only women in warm climates
would walk barefoot over
the bridged backs of alligators, whose jaws
jilt open like badly fastened handbags.

Women in warm climates
can scut an oyster
from its briny box, and with a sharp spoon
unsex the whiskered artichoke.

The black knot and scroll of balconies
must have been built
for women in warm climates—
and verandahs where the winds splash
all afternoon, and fans that dangle
their headfirst petals on a stiff stem.

In the fat lap of summer,
they practice
the principles of inertia, largo of
moss and womb and dream.
And would your touch
stir the heavy syrup through their hearts
to sweeten them, or your name become
the smoke and smoulder in their blood?
Women in warm climates
slake their lips
at the madder of a moist mouth,
unloosing from the deep end of desire
smiles that ripen in the night.

It's Always Warmer by the Fire, When the Wind Blows Cold

You can still remember the honeysuckle belles of LSU
And the party boys from Ole Miss, back in the retrofuture,

All your faults perfected in their infancy. Who would mind
The occasional handcuff, the feral kiss, in that dirty paradise?

They say that catfish get fatter near the bottomlands. They say
The sweetest grapes hide their luster deep inside the shade.

But a sundial cuts through the day like a sharkfin,
And every hour's a small postmortem on the hour gone before.

Now all your dreams of vague acres under a southern sky
Stay stuck in this unforgiving snow. Citizen of the withered spark,

Refugee approaching the cold border, why don't you
Stir these embers in the firecrib, and see what good that does?

Narcissus as Is

Always myself, whatever waters I look into,
I keep my head
Above the flow, and never let the current
Carry me away.
However strong the stream, I want it still.

However strong the stream, I want it. Still,
I sometimes long
For pools so small no winds will sway them
On my face,
Tired of staring at the drift of things.

Tired of staring at the drift of things,
I could see
Beyond my eyes to all that springs below
And rises here,
A glass that goes down deep and bears me up.

A glass that goes down deep and bears me up—
Break it now,
This calm whose end is ice, and not the rush
That keeps me
Always myself, whatever waters I look into.

And in the Afternoons I Botanized

Where we sat, on the flagstone terrace behind the house,
Gin cooling in the spill of civilian twilight, ice cubes
Doing the deadman's float, with air rough to the touch,
The birch leaves blown yellow, in the lacerating shape of spades,
And thin boughs heaving a little with the season's sickness,
You said: We've come to calamity and the end of things.
Even the bees are weary, and the honey heavy, the petals depressed.
The wars you lose last longer than the wars you win.

And it was true. I could feel the same breeze, pallbearer of the birch,
October heading the dark cortège. Where others might trace
Lifelines in the palm, I read, on the back of my hand,
Liver spots like annotations on a last draft. No goldfinch
Flew to the feeder of wild seed; in the worked earth,
No chipmunk burrowed at the sweet root of the bulb.
And yet, in the mornings, fruit still hung fresh and firm,
Dew-dappled apples, frost smoke thick on the ground.

You said: If that crusty north-of-Boston poet had put us
In a poem, would we stand stiff as figures from a snow globe,
The trees bowed down around us, each branch bent
With the weight of meditation, the cling of imagery? Or would we
Lean on a worm fence, blood stropped in the heart,
Between us those moments where anger rubs on injury—
The tone medium wry, the pace pieced out in syllables
That stick in the throat, the ache of everything unsaid?

Well, better that than chintz and chimes, some teapot dame
Who'd make us talk on stilts, or in the weak repeats of
Rondeaus and rondels, French inventions that sound like
Girl groups from the Sixties. Would you rather lose yourself
In the cold echoes of Eliot, his vaulted voice dry as
Stone commencements at the graveside? Or find yourself
Edged out by the muscle of music in late Yeats?
We'll take our own line, broken, with a grain of sense and salt.

But no words slow down the dirt. And these drinks,
Essence of emptiness from the juniper berry, can't bring back

A duckweb spray of maple paddling in the slipstreams of spring,
Or the flowering crab, or panicles of japonica. You said:
At 47, I'm in my prime numbers, indivisible, entered
Only by myself and one other—odd and middling and absolute—
The mind still testing out every hedge against death,
The short con and the long shot, the bet called on the come.

It's no wonder we nail our days to the wall, and hang
Distractions of the calendar, slick colors over the Xed-out box:
Gaunt barge of Venice in the green canals; the love knot puzzles of
Women in the pink; and from Monet, the blue and purple pulp of water
    blooms.
So all our albums fail the past: pictures of picnics and the rose ribbons of
Girls dozy under the summer oak; your unparalleled apparel,
That dress the shade of bittersweet; and my brand-new panama,
Black band around the crown, hat like an elegy for the head.

You said: If we were characters cast in a play, could we choose
Some comedy written in the wit of Restoration, and call ourselves
Lord and Lady Vainhope, or the Fallshorts of a London season?
We'd stumble through contraptions of the plot, dull but not despised,
Wanting only to be better than we were, the axis of laughter
Set spinning by the jibes of gentlemen, the housemaid's joke.
A frump of mangled language, a squire's fat harrumph,
We'd ride out the raillery, redeemed as the footlights dimmed.

It might be worse. The Greeks would strap us both behind
A mask of agony, and raise, behind us both, tall columns
Glazed with gore, history dripping from the choral odes.
I'd rather see myself aggrieved in Italy, young and speaking
Blank verse in the twisted streets, a moon-mad lover
Swooning over poison and a toy sword. These days,
They'd heap us unrehearsed in garbage cans, two bums
Practicing their rap before the bottom and the silence fell.

And what had the light left? A Chinese banner of a cloud
Burned across the sun, scarlet and gold of pennants at half-mast,

As the last glow lowered. Strung out among the spikes of dahlia,
A spider's tension stripped the air, a tripwire brushing
The dawdly fuss of a butterfly. You said: Sometimes I feel
Like a rabbit in the brightbeams, or a statue packed in sawdust,
Chained and crated and stowed away. How could I move,
Always made to bear up the dead weight of the self?

In this state of the ladybug and the buckeye whose shell
Battles back the winter like a scaled-down mace, where each
Politician and professor fights for his own empire of ideas,
Theories that colonize the brain, we've reached a common level:
Freaks under the tent, as damaged as Patty the Penguin Girl
Or the Dancing Pinheads, bad goods in the chromosomes, and pain
The price of admission, as the babies know, dangling brow-down inside
    the thighs,
Their first look at the world bloody and the wrong way up.

If we're all born, as Augustine said, between the feces and the urine,
We have a bone to pick with anatomy. And what was *his* problem—
Too much time spent cramped under the pelvic shelf? You can tell,
On every page, his pleasures in confession, nosing out the rank
And the dry rot, the mossy odors of the soul. I'd like to hear him
Alive and in Vienna, knees tucked up on the couch, as the dream doctor
Probed below the belt, fingers wrinkling in his beard: Vell, Herr
    Augustine,
Vunce more about your mother, and that voice calling from the vall.

Every rebel bred in appointed peace, every child squeezed from
Some squall in the loins, looks on love like a maggot,
That soft surgeon cleaning out the open festers where they hurt.
Who wouldn't sigh to live among the satisfied, in a mansion of
White linen, high polish, white paint, the windows unfolding on
A square of fountains from which the waters leaped in chandeliers?
All those who rise from rags to rages have had their infancy
Where the ends are mean and no gods ease the difficult middle.

You said: It comes clear now, that midsummer month of rain,
And the mushrooms over the lawn, large and limp, spread flat

Like severed ears listening for the next tremor, the resurrection of the
     flesh.
In the darkness, after the storms, everything sounded too loud, too close.
What could I do? There's only so much the rain can erase,
In natural baptism or new flood. That ooze draining through the night,
That rush and suck of water on the run—it frightened me,
As if heaven once more had breathed into the slippery limbs of mud.

By that stand of asters and the late mallow, where we sat
Like monks gone blind in the margin of manuscripts, and heard
Those arguments whose laws lead to the great Therefore, our hands
Stretched and met, both of us ghostly in the pale stains,
The mineral wastes of moonlight, deep dredge of shadows beneath our
     feet.
You said: Is there no way out of this helpless evidence?
And I put my shaken fingers to your lips, that wound
The words come from, worn down, drifting, like leaves in a sleepy wind.

Zero with an Arrow, Zero with a Cross

When you came dripping in from the rain,
Sundress soaked against you like a mind
Contemplating its own work and erasure,

I wore nothing but two hats: a cap, all wool,
To keep my thinking warm; and my fedora,
That low felt shadow on the flesh.

If I should say how much I like
Your flameproof lips, and the way your tongue
Slides over the salt on a dizzy rim,

If I should praise an eye that's absolute
And a heart's high tide, all the tufts and pouts
And sockets of the body, the whole shebang,

With no advance apologies, no time for distant critics
Or the tribal repetitions of rebuke, why should that
Make me a bird's breakfast on a wet lawn,

Or something scraped from the bottom of a sole?
In the mist and slippage of our years,
This age of theory when a theory of age

Means more mass, less energy, a slow
Downdraft and backstream into matter,
Who would live on a roughage of sawdust

Or by those arguments that answer silk
With floursacks? Plant trees when you're young,
And annuals after forty. While there's still

Something left to be desired, I'll bare my head
To the second wind of love, and breathe
Hard in the charities of your soft touch.

First Night 2000

After the spangles
And the stems of fire, the fray of sparks
And smoke rolling on the west wind,
We feel again
The ice under our feet, the dry air
That cracks this first kiss in the dark
Of a thousand years,
The crowds already driving back
Through blue fumes of their own exhaust,
Until we're left
Alone in the new night, just two,
Two, before the nothing that outnumbers us.

Anecdotal Evidence

Love, love, how can you
Keep us locked against
Each other, two hearts
Caught in a fast freeze,
A press that closes off
Even the light hard wrung
From the wintry warp of darkness?

I've heard how the sea-struck *Terror*,
Its sails short-winded, had docked
In the polar floes, the ice
Spliced so tight it stove
The bow in, buckled the deck
And the bulkheads, and made
Timbers weep with turpentine—

And how, when summer broke
The cold's blockade, this ship
Set its course across
The crippled waters, seams
Sprung at the bilge line, canvas
Aglare in the gales and calm,
Heaving its warm way home.

Son et Lumiere

When sun quickens the glass and wakes the day,
Even a stale heel of bread will dazzle you,

And dust rising like glitter around your feet.
You once thought there was heartbreak

In a pair of shoes half-hidden under the empty bed,
In a ticket, torn in two, on the bedside table.

That was before the light of summer afternoon
Ripened on the pillow and warmed the sheets,

Before the open window brought in from next door
The scent of dinner and someone humming

With the radio, the shadow sound of someone
Near and alone, on the other side of yourself.

Spring Offensive

Gentle Love,
Draw forth thy wounding dart
—JOHN DOWLAND

That baby with a bow
stands cocked on one foot in the garden,
desire strung out to the breaking point

and aimed at the spray
fluting up from the birdbath, no deeper
than the small well between your breasts.

Or does it point against
that far target, shadow of the big hand
closing over the slow circle of the sundial?

No one seems to mind
his full frontal pouch and prod,
a bud too antique or infantile to bloom.

Beebalm and the butterfly bush
send out new shoots; starlings lift off
like loose shutters that clatter in the wind.

If you would let yourself
come open to this kiss, what tongue
would wag the news or clack a nunnish no?

That boy, unfledged as his arrow,
dimples down on us, his lips releasing
the archaic smile that only stone bestows.

Elegant Gathering in the Apricot Garden

—HANDSCROLL BY XIE HUAN

Not paradise, no windfall scent of apple
Or jeweled evasions of the snake,

But this garden on a silk scroll, six feet
Of tint and ink, and five figures

At ease inside a rough pavilion,
Screen of leafy branches laced around

A pale lattice of bamboo. On a bamboo pole,
A boy holds up a painted cloth, its loose end

Settled in some elder's lap. Whatever the old man
Sees there and says, it seems to please

The graybeard next to him, looking on,
Hands buried in the broad sleeves of his robe.

Behind them, in gowns of pink and moss,
Two others wait, one standing

With a scroll half-open, and one
Seated at a low table, his brush poised

As if to take dictation, to make his mark
Against the emptiness unrolled before him.

No fruit, no ripe imperatives of flesh
Seduce the palate, in this landscape

Too serene for anything but muted shades,
This quiet gathering of men

Composed in cool silk, far below
The high tension of the stars

No one can see, and somewhere beyond
The ache and panic of desire.

After the Snows

I'm not in love with
The spring trees, limbs of the pear and apple
Still thin, and the first shy buds
Barely there, pink and pale—
Victoriana of the wan nudes.

Late April makes the bluebell rise,
And the hyacinth, a sweet
Cluster of curls
Reeling the cool air, though it cannot
Stir my sullen blood.

But you, when the ice slides
From thick to thaw, and the noon sun
Softens all the torments of this earth, you
Bring me back by one touch
Of your forgiving hand.

In Another Life

—for Gerald Stern

In another life,
I will learn to give myself to the litany of the dispossessed,
To make novenas to Our Lady of Nothing and her handsome son;
I will attach retractable wheels to the bottom beam of the cross
And drag it like a suitcase through all the airports of America,
Rolling up the bonus miles on my Frequent Sufferer's card.

In another life,
I will enter a twelve-step program for the five stages of grief;
I will abandon the blinds of denial, the old tricks of addiction,
And shut down the two glands that keep me from control: the pituitary
With its lust for lebensraum, and the adrenal pumping out hormones like a
    fire hose.
I will put myself under the knife and the clamps and the black stitch
That reroutes the eyes, connecting the optical nerve to the tear duct,
That I might weep more freely for everything I see.

In another life,
I will dispose of the fears that seep over me like barrels of industrial waste,
And the shame that turns my most secluded truth into lies slipping down the
    lips
As if I were made to drink communion wine from a dribble cup;
I will translate *goodbye* as *blasphemy*, *hello* as *mattress*,
And let the lamentations of anaphora be misconstrued as praise.

In another life,
I will compose a eulogy for all the minor animals of earth and air—
Moles drowned in their tunnels, mice run down by their own perpetual
    motion,
A cricket caught up in the ratchet of its decibels, and the mockingbird,
That virtuoso whose voice flows back and forth between the rapids of
    vernacular
And the aqueducts of Latin, its feathers gone gray as a poet trying too hard
To steer and brake the accelerated sonnets of this noisy shift.

In another life,
I will comfort the video junkies, victims of the joystick and the data-rape;

I will romance the dowager matrons with their pearls and Pekinese, satin
    mums on a satin hat;
I will ease the fevers and the leaky sleep that waken the night nurse,
Her fantasies teased by the unnatural science of charms and alchemy.

In another life,
Somewhere in back of the above, just past the exit to the past,
I'll carry a torch and a tune for Gertrude, putting a hillbilly spin
On *The Trail of the Lonesome Pine*, that song she most sighed for, sharing
The sheet music with her lover, Alice of the gypsy drapes and the soft
    mustache;
And I'll speak in menu Italian to Dante Alighieri, whose map of hell
Can't be complete until he's bottomed out at Mario's Eateria in the Mall:
A double bucket of lasagna, with extra garlic on the shovel bread.

In another life,
I will stop saluting flags soaked in the blood of children,
Blood running in stripes like the last inch of daylight
Drained from the horizon, above which the stars advance in ranks,
An arsenal of edges keen enough to cut through the small moans and
    screams.

In another life,
I will not worry over the low bubbling in my lungs, the feel of
Something deep on the rise, a clot of old ooze stopping the breath,
Tar in the bellows, sludge in the pipeline, coughing up the plugs and hockets
That block the air's path to the words trembling under my tongue.

In another life,
I will bow down to bar stools, and raise up the glass that is always
Empty to the top, to the brim of invisible vodka, hard proof
That even a blind potato can be king in the country of the bloodshot eye.

In another life,
I will study the late pages of Malory, full of flaws and horses
And the pure who sally out beyond the shaken limits of their innocence,
And a stone on which someone has scrawled, in French letters too large
To fit inside the lopsided heart, *Lancelot loves G. out of measure,*

And the errors of a second sad king betrayed by his disciples, hung up
On the hilt of his sword, blade of an even temper and a broken point.

In another life,
I will attend the autopsy of this life, a white room where they peel
The shadow from its corpse, twisting on itself in a jar of clear liquid,
A clue in case of foul play, in case the widow wants another look
At the dark profile, a negative in its acid bath, a slur
From which all events leading to this cold moment can be traced,
In case there is a case, a claim made to indemnify the damned.

In another life,
If the wings don't work, if the halo draws down the shocks and sizzle
Stored up in a thunderstorm, I'll take the shuttle flight to heaven,
Booked standby into panic class, my mind a matter of gin over gravity,
Rivets rattling like spare change in the air pockets, and each cloud a speed
    bump in the blue.

In another life,
I will scrape the flypaper poems on which the dead details still stick,
And start from scratch, from the hand idling over odds and ends,
Far from the writers conference and the Spanish manacles of grammar,
Taking from Vallejo his pain and compassion, Incan secrets in the ink,
And from Neruda, that waterwheel of the wild Americas, taking his
    cascadence,
Surge and pull over the tall crest, until it all falls loose,
That snarl in the soul, that kink in the cramped coilage of the lines.

In another life,
I will not deny my pagan sympathies for wheat and the winesap apple,
Or my need for dissonance and backtalk, stutter of rain on a tin roof;
I will model myself on that old goose who lived in a shoe, and make my
    home
In the third stomach of a ruminant, among the gas and the enzymes, where
    anything goes.
What then will be left for me to desire or confess?
In another life, not far from this one,
I will love you like a lick of flame on the brows of wobbly apostles,

Because you kiss with lips plush enough to line the bronze bed of my
    coffin,
Because your hot heart can melt even the polar overwhelmings of the
    mind,
Because no spirit but yours comes out so open in this grave age,
Naked as a new shoot pushed up in the stir of wet and light.

Ab Ovo

So this is love, more or less:
Sucking the sleepbreath from her kiss
Before the pillows cool; letting the infant
Shake its first fist at the shadows
Bent over it; not looking down
The deep sleeve of God to see
What dove he's conjured up this time,
Its neck knotted in a noose of blood.

And if less, if the folktales tell us
With their griefs and felonies, their jinxs and hints,
That wise virgins must choose between being
Virgin or wise, that the hero's heart must
Push its pluck against a life both
Lucky and unjust—well, what spell would
Slow the breakage from egg to grave,
If not love, whatever name it came to:
Third wish of the third son,
Or curse, or quirk, or clamor in the bone.

Solo in the Skeleton Key

Who would plant, in this stony ground, narcissus and love-lies-bleeding?
It's too late to be young among the primitives. Winter withers the stalks.

The air reeks of it, decay and the odor of innocence gone to seed.
The time for riots and tattoos is over. Who dances the Dazzle now, or the
     Swerve?

Long before the armada and the asp, Antony must have tired of Cleopatra,
Those heavy breasts, that midnight skin, a name that thickened in his
     throat.

In the heat from eating an incandescent pepper, there's neither passion
Nor apocalypse, just tongues in hell, just retching and the runs.

What honey comes from old drones? Forget the hoodoo and the holy water.
Pray only in Jerusalem, at the Church of Our Lady of the Spasm.

Love's no trick of ecstasy, no lightning strike in the mind. Each new child
Struggles out, bloody and stunned, one more last chance to get it right.

ACKNOWLEDGMENTS

I gratefully acknowledge the following magazines, in which many of these poems first were published, some in slightly different versions:

Alligator Juniper: "Coupling on the Edge of Entropy," "Eastern Winter Time"; *Arroyo Literary Review*: "Dating Cassandra"; *Bellingham Review*: "Homage to John Ashbery"; *5 AM*: "95% of Love Is Half of What You Want," "Unrequited Dialogue by Moonlight"; *Georgetown Review*: "Ab Ovo"; *Georgia Review*: "Category Error," "Exhaustion," "Spoils"; *Gettysburg Review*: "Hermetically Sealed," "Mythos of Honey and Brine," "The Sexual, as Opposed to What," "Toast"; *Iowa Review*: "Narcissus as Is"; *Journal*: "No, and I Wouldn't Name My Cat Cleopatra, Either," "Spring Offensive"; *Laurel Review*: "Fantasia on a Phrase from Don DeLillo," "Zero with an Arrow, Zero with a Cross"; *Marlboro Review*: "Getting It Straight"; *Mid-American Review*: "Prayer from the Back Pew"; *Missouri Review*: "Regression Analysis"; *New Ohio Review*: "Downloading the Meltdown," "Solo in the Skeleton Key"; *North American Review*: "Low Tide on the Sunset Coast"; *OnEarth*: "After the Snows"; *Parnassus*: "And in the Afternoons I Botanized"; *Poetry*: "In Another Life," "Midnight at the *Club Imaginaire*"; *Poetry Northwest*: "Anecdotal Evidence"; *Shenandoah*: "Evenings Homesick for the Absolute," "Group Therapy for the Bards," "Petitions to the Tenderloin"; *Southern California Anthology*: "Amo, Amas, Amat"; *Subtropics*: "Mad in Manhattan"; *Texas Observer*: "First Night 2000"; *West Branch*: "Elegant Gathering in the Apricot Garden."

"And in the Afternoons I Botanized" was reprinted in *The Best American Poetry 2000*, edited by Rita Dove (New York: Scribner, 2000), and in *Poetry Daily: 366 Poems from the World's Most Popular Poetry Website*, edited by Diane Boller, Don Selby, and Chryss Yost (Napierville, IL: Soundbooks, 2003).

I would like to thank the University of Akron for a sabbatical leave during which I completed an earlier version of this book. Some of these poems were given guidance by Mary Biddinger, Bob Dial, Tom Dukes, William Greenway, Jeanne Hulstine, Michelle Moore, Jay Robinson, Jana Russ, and Chris White.

For help with making crucial adjustments to the book, I owe a special debt to Lynn Powell, my best critic.